A LOCAL'S GUIDE TO
BLOODLINE

BRAD BERTELLI   **DAVID SLOAN**

PHANTOM PRESS
KEY WEST

Editorial services: DorothyDrennen.com

Inquiries: david@phantompress.com

ISBN: 978-0-9831671-9-8

HOW TO USE

WHAT TO EXPECT
This guide is comprehensive and includes most of the film locations in the Florida Keys from Season 2 and Season 3. Some of the locations are fantastic stops that were featured multiple times and are easily recognizable. Others appeared briefly and are unremarkable apart from their Bloodline affiliation. Just pick and choose locations from your favorite scenes.

MILE MARKERS
Most directions in the Florida Keys involve Mile Markers. Mile Marker 0 is in Key West. Mile Marker 108 is in Key Largo. To get a sense of what Mile Marker a location is near, remove the last three digits from its listed address.

OCEANSIDE AND BAYSIDE
Local directions will often include *Oceanside* or *Bayside*. When driving along the Overseas Highway, the southbound land represents the Bayside or Florida Bay side of the highway. The northbound lane represents the Atlantic Ocean side or Oceanside of the highway.

FIRST FEATURED
The *First Featured* section for each location tells you when and where the location appeared so you can watch the scene on your phone or tablet.

KNOW BEFORE YOU GO
While most locations are accessible and open to the public, some are private or just don't have time to deal with sightseers. Check the *Getting There* section for each location before you go so you know what to expect.

SPOILER ALERT
This book contains plot details from Seasons 1, 2 and 3.

LOCATION LIST

1. SAM'S HIDEAWAY
2. EVERGLADES ALLIGATOR FARM
3. GILBERT'S RESORT
4. ROAD TO NOWHERE
5. GILBERT'S RESORT DRIVE UNDERPASS
6. BUZZARD'S ROOST
7. KEVIN'S DRIVE
8. TOM THUMB
9. DUSENBURY CREEK
10. PINK PLAZA
11. THE JUICE HOUSE
12. ALLEN-BEYER FUNERAL HOME
13. FLORIDA KEYS SHOOTING CLUB
14. KEY LARGO FISHERIES
15. MOLASSES REEF
16. DENNY'S LATIN CAFE
17. THE PILOT HOUSE
18. MRS. MAC'S KITCHEN
19. WYLAND'S WHALING WALL
20. ISLAND GRILL MANDALAY
21. DAIRY QUEEN
22. HARRY HARRIS PARK
23. KEVIN'S GUNPOINT DRIVE
24. TOILET SEAT CUT
25. OLD TAVERNIER RESTAURANT

LOCATION LIST

26. CORAL SHORES HIGH SCHOOL
27. SAN PEDRO CHURCH
28. BALI HAI
29. MONROE COUNTY DETENTION CENTER
30. PLANTATION KEY COURTHOUSE
31. FOUNDERS PARK AMPHITHEATER
32. FOUNDER'S PARK
33. MARCO'S HOUSE
34. HARBOR LIGHTS MOTEL
35. POSTCARD INN MARINA
36. WHALE HARBOR CHAIN GANG
37. ACE HARDWARE
38. PRODUCTION LOT
39. CORAL BAY MARINA
40. WOODY'S
41. OCEAN SOTHEBY'S INTERNATIONAL REALTY
42. PIONEER CEMETERY AT CHEECA LODGE
43. THE MOORINGS RESORT & SPA
44. FISHBONE CHARTERS
45. BANYAN TREE
46. PALMS OF ISLAMORADA
47. INDIAN KEY
48. ERIC'S HIDEOUT
49. CALOOSA COVE
50. LONG KEY TRANSFER STATION

MAP

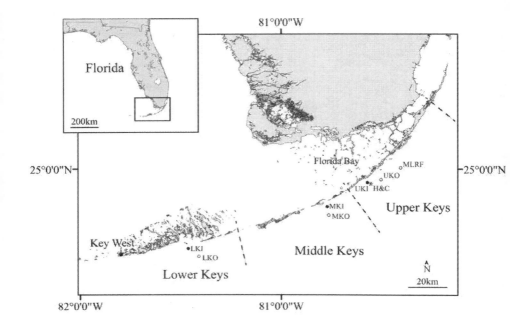

Most film locations are in the Upper Keys section of the above map. This section represents Islamorada and Key Largo. Locations in this guide are listed geographically from north to south, with number 1 being the northernmost location. Mile Markers for each city are listed below.

KEY LARGO: 108-91
ISLAMORADA: 90-66
MARATHON: 65-40
BIG PINE KEY: 39-9
KEY WEST: 8-0

THE WATER LETS YOU IN

BLOODLINE THEME BY BOOK OF FEARS

YOUNG MAN GOES OUT LOOKING
FOR THE DIAMOND IN THE SEA.
OLD MAN ROWS HIS BOAT TO SHORE
AND FALLS ON TWISTED KNEES.

AND YOU'LL DROWN BEFORE
THE WATER LETS YOU IN...
YOU'LL DROWN BEFORE
THE WATER LETS YOU IN...

THE FEELING THAT I FEAR THE MOST
IS THE ONE THAT FOLLOWS ME.
ALL ACROSS THE STARRY COAST
FROM SEA TO DYING SEA. IT SAYS...

YOU'LL DROWN BEFORE
THE WATER LETS YOU IN...
YOU'LL DROWN BEFORE
THE WATER LETS YOU IN...

I THINK THE THING I'VE WANTED MOST
WAS JUST NEVER MEANT TO BE.
A THOUSAND WAVES, A THOUSAND GHOSTS
THEIR SORROWS FOLLOW ME.

AND YOU'LL DROWN BEFORE
THE WATER LETS YOU IN...
YOU'LL DROWN BEFORE
THE WATER LETS YOU IN...

OH HORRIBLE, OH HORRIBLE DAY.

1

SAM'S HIDEAWAY
750 S KROME AVE
FLORIDA CITY
(305) 246-9512

THE SCENE

Meg calls Marco from outside this bar and apologizes to him. She lets him know that she leaked info about Aguirre, but kept him out of it. Marco calls her a liar and makes it clear that they no longer have a personal relationship. Meg begs. Marco hangs up on her.

BEHIND THE SCENE

Sam's Hideaway has a sign on the wall claiming that Sam's is "The Oldest Southernmost Tavern on the Mainland USA." Visitors are welcomed with a mural featuring two dolphins jumping over a frosty mug. Inside you find a classic dive bar that makes you feel right at home.

GETTING THERE

From US1 South in Florida City, turn right on Krome Avenue immediately after you pass the RaceTrac gas station. The bar will be just up the road on your left.

FIRST FEATURED

Part 23 | 41:13

LOCAL BUZZ

The coconut telegraph says that Linda Cardellini (Meg) filmed her parts for season 3 outside of the Florida Keys because she was concerned about Zika.

2

EVERGLADES
ALLIGATOR FARM
40351 SW 192ND AVE
FLORIDA CITY
EVERGLADES.COM | (305) 247-2628

THE SCENE
Season 3 opens with Kevin fleeing Marco's house and John driving down a dark highway. In between these scenes there are shots of an alligator lurking slowly beneath the water. Later, John hits the gator with his truck.

BEHIND THE SCENE
Located near the entrance of Everglades National Park, this is South Florida's oldest alligator farm and contains more than 2000 alligators. They offer airboat tours, alligator shows, snake shows, and an alligator feeding demonstration.

GETTING THERE
From US1 South, turn right onto SW 344th Street, then left at the iconic Robert Is Here fruit and vegetable stand onto 192nd Ave. The road ends in the parking lot of the alligator farm. There are alternate routes, so use GPS on this one if you can.

FIRST FEATURED
Part 24 | 2:11

BOAT DRINKS
Kyle Chandler *(John)* and Jamie McShane *(Eric)* took a boat out to Alligator Reef during their time in the Keys. While there, they drank a 12-pack of beer and watched sharks swim around.

3

GILBERT'S RESORT
107900 OVERSEAS HIGHWAY
KEY LARGO
GILBERTSRESORT.COM | (305) 451-1133

THE SCENE

John and his daughter are having lunch at Gilbert's. Ozzy buys their lunch, then Ozzy and John have an awkward encounter. Ozzy tells John he is staying at the Red Reef Motel in room number seven, then, hinting at Danny, asks John if he has ever been there. John's guard is going up, so he tries to get Ozzy's name—but Ozzy walks away.

BEHIND THE SCENE

Known as the first and last stop in the Florida Keys, Gilbert's started out in 1903 as a fishing camp. Today they are famous for their giant Tiki bar, live entertainment, and Keys casual dining. The drinks are cold, too. Shoes are optional.

GETTING THERE

Take the Gilbert's Resort Drive exit off of the Jewfish Creek Bridge at Mile Marker 107.9. The resort will be obvious.

FIRST FEATURED

Part 18 | 48:21

SHAKEN, NOT STIRRED

Kyle Chandler's *(John)* family jokes that he was conceived after too many martinis on New Year's Eve. In homage, his middle name is Martin.

4

ROAD TO NOWHERE
JEWFISH CREEK BRIDGE
107800 OVERSEAS HIGHWAY
KEY LARGO

THE SCENE

John Rayburn sits in his pick-up truck at the end of this dead-end street, surrounded by mangroves, as his speech announcing his intention to run for mayor plays in his head. He tears up a photograph of the dead drug dealer, Rafi Quintana, which he stole from evidence as the last line of his speech plays: "Human nature needs to be nurtured and policed so as to save us from ourselves. "

BEHIND THE SCENE

The highway to the Keys originally ran across the Card Sound Bridge. During World War II, the Navy in Key West wanted improved access to the mainland, so the Overseas Highway was rerouted onto the former railroad right of way. The original Jewfish Creek beam bridge opened to traffic in 1944. The current bridge was built in 2008. The road to nowhere was likely part of a failed development project.

GETTING THERE

The road to nowhere can be seen from the Jewfish Creek Bridge off to the east shortly after the bridge starts when you are heading north. Exit before the bridge to drive down the road.

FIRST FEATURED

Part 15 | 54:42

BORN TO BE WILD

A motorcycle was Kyle Chandler's *(John)* main form of transportation while he was filming in the Keys.

5

GILBERT'S RESORT
DRIVE UNDERPASS
107800 OVERSEAS HIGHWAY
KEY LARGO

THE SCENE

John is featured in a dream sequence. He believes he is driving with his mother. She tells him that Eric tried to escape and was shot. John tells her he killed Danny. She says they have all wanted to kill Danny at one time or another. They look at each other. A horn honks as she drifts lanes. Their vehicle flips and it appears Sally is dead.

BEHIND THE SCENE

Gilbert's Resort lost a lot of business when the new raised bridge was installed. The state would not put signage on the road directing people to the resort, so they changed the name of the road that the exit was on. The state had no choice but to put up signs for Gilbert's Resort Drive.

GETTING THERE

This scene was filmed on the northbound exit of Gilbert's Resort Drive off of the Overseas Highway as the road curves just before you go under the bridge. The exit is near Mile Marker 107.8.

FIRST FEATURED

Part 32 | 6:53

COAL MINER'S DAUGHTER

Sissy Spacek's daughter, singer/songwriter Schuyler Fisk was scheduled to play at a Bloodline cast party. She lost her voice, so Sissy filled in on vocals.

6

THE BUZZARD'S ROOST
21 GARDEN COVE DRIVE
KEY LARGO
BUZZARDSROOSTKEYLARGO.COM | (305) 453-3746

THE SCENE
John and Diana dine here with Mike Gallagher and his wife, old friends from Boston. Mike encourages John to join him in the private security sector for triple the pay. Outside, Mike makes a pass at Diana and kisses her. She does not immediately resist.

BEHIND THE SCENE
The Buzzard's Roost has been around since 1959 and offers great waterfront dining in Key Largo. Rumor has it that the site was once popular with smugglers. Today it is known for a great wine selection, homemade desserts, and Sunday brunch. The dinner in the scene was held inside. Scenes were also filmed at the Tiki bar.

GETTING THERE
Located just off Mile Marker 106.5 Oceanside. Take Garden Cove Drive to Cayman Lane and take a right. The restaurant will be on your left.

FIRST FEATURED
Part 31 | 15:49

VALLEY FORGE
Mark Valley *(Mike Gallagher)* graduated West Point in 1987. He wrote the one-man show, "Walls, Wars & Whiskey" about his experiences in the military.

7

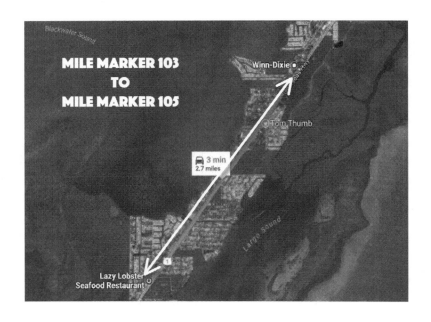

KEVIN'S DRIVE
MILE MARKER 103 TO 105
KEY LARGO

THE SCENE

Kevin drives north on this stretch of the Overseas Highway looking frustrated and confused. A car honks at him as it passes. Kevin flips them the bird. He changes radio stations rapidly until he settles on Billie Holiday singing *God Bless the Child*. The song calms him down.

BEHIND THE SCENE

Not much to talk about behind the scene here. But we will tell you that the best way to amp up this stretch of highway, a stretch that you will be driving anyway, is to download *God Bless the Child* and play it while you drive where Kevin did. Trust us. We did it.

GETTING THERE

This stretch runs north starting close to the Lazy Lobster near Mile Marker 103 and ending near the Winn Dixie by Mile Marker 105.

FIRST FEATURED

Part 27 | 23:41

WASTING AWAY AGAIN

Norbert Leo Butz *(Kevin)* joined Jimmy Buffett in singing Margaritaville on stage at the Green Turtle Inn while he was down here during filming.

8

TOM THUMB
104701 OVERSEAS HIGHWAY
KEY LARGO
(305)451-3944

THE SCENE

Kevin is filling up with gas at this Tom Thumb convenience store when his mother calls. He tells her all the news is good that day and that they are going to have the baby's christening on Sunday. He asks if they can have the party at the inn. Sally hesitates. Kevin gets upset with her and asks when the last time was she had a party?

BEHIND THE SCENE

Tom Thumb is a family-owned and operated chain of gas stations and convenience stores that spans from Fort Lauderdale to Key West. Their goal is "Fast, Fresh, and Friendly." They have been around since 1964.

GETTING THERE

Tom Thumb is located at Mile Marker 104.7 Oceanside. Watch for "Tom" in big red letters.

FIRST FEATURED

Part 27 | 19:05

JAM BAND

The Norbert Leo Butz Band played at the 23rd annual Bay Jam in Islamorada. The played on the same stage where Marco's funeral took place.

9

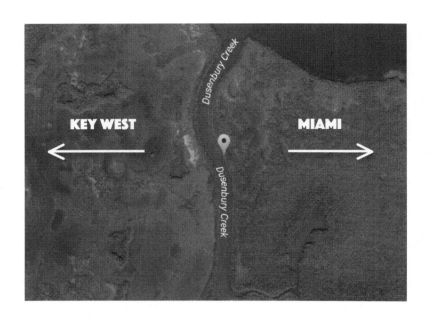

KEY WEST ← | → MIAMI

Dusenbury Creek

DUSENBURY CREEK
(VIA FLORIDA BAY OUTFITTERS)
104050 OVERSEAS HIGHWAY
KEY LARGO
PADDLEFLORIDAKEYS.COM | (305) 451-3018

THE SCENE
John tells Meg of his plans to frame Eric. They try to figure out where Eric is and John recalls that they used to go down and party in the mangroves near Mile Marker 100. Meg remembers that is was a shack on Dusenbury Creek.

BEHIND THE SCENE
Dusenbury Creek hosts some of the best mangrove tunnels in the Florida Keys. All types of wildlife call the area home. Though the area would be a great place for a hideaway party shack, Dusenbury Creek was only used as a reference in Bloodline. The shack used for filming is located at Robbie's Marina in Islamorada.

GETTING THERE
Kayak is the best way to explore Dusenbury Creek. The closest launch and rental facility is Florida Bay Outfitters located at Mile Marker 104 right next door the Caribbean Club, Bayside.

FIRST FEATURED
Part 26 | 27:02

I'LL DRINK TO THAT
On playing a lush, Linda Cardellini *(Meg)* says, "It's always slightly daunting, but it's really fun too."

10

PINK PLAZA
103400 OVERSEAS HIGHWAY
KEY LARGO

THE SCENE
Chelsea meets John in the parking lot of this strip mall. She tells him that Eric is falling apart. Chelsea asks if there is anything John can do to help Eric. John says no. Chelsea shows John a photograph of young Eric and Danny with Danny's arm in a cast. She asks what happened, then offers the photo to John. He says he doesn't want it. She asks one more time for help. John pulls away.

BEHIND THE SCENE
Pink Plaza is a staple of the Florida Keys landscape with 57,773 square feet of mixed use retail over two stories. It features on of the busiest West Marine's in the nation. This scene was filmed close to the main entrance directly across the street from ProTech e2.

GETTING THERE
Watch for the sign with the neon pink flamingo near Mile Marker 103.4 Bayside. The strip plaza is hard to miss.

FIRST FEATURED
Part 29 | 28:10

SWAN SONG
"I'm not happy it ended, but I'm glad it ended where it did." – *Kyle Chandler*

11

JUICE HOUSE
103200 OVERSEAS HIGHWAY
KEY LARGO
305-451-4270

THE SCENE
Ozzy Delvecchio receives a Cuban coffee at the walk-up window of the Juice House as he talks on his cell phone. As he walks by the front door he sees a "Rayburn For Sheriff" sign and says, "That could be a good thing. A *real* good thing."

BEHIND THE SCENE
The Juice House is known for their Cuban food. They have over 100 menu items and 20+ coffees, smoothies, and juices.

GETTING THERE
On the Overseas Highway at Mile Marker 103.2, look for the bright yellow awning in Central Plaza.

FIRST FEATURED
Part 16, 28:58

LOL
John Leguizamo *(Ozzy)* started out as a stand-up comic doing the New York nightclub circuit in 1984.

12

ALLEN-BEYER
FUNERAL HOME
101640 OVERSEAS HIGHWAY
KEY LARGO
BEYERFUNERAL.NET | (305) 451-1444

THE SCENE
Chelsea calls John from this funeral home during John's dream sequence. She says she is leaving. He says he needs to come see her, but she says it is not a good idea. Eric is lying dead in a casket. John says he is sorry, but Chelsea tells him it is too late for that. Nolan and Sarah add to the creep factor.

BEHIND THE SCENE
The Beyer Funeral Home was founded by Harry and Marilyn Beyer in 1971. They opened the business in the front half of an old hardware store. The place has always been a family run business. Today it is operated by Tony and Jacqui Allen.

GETTING THERE
Watch for the name in large print on the awning at Mile Marker 101.6 Bayside. If visiting this location, always be respectful of funerals and the dead.

FIRST FEATURED
Part 32 | 38:31

NET WORTH
While launching his acting career, Jamie McShane (Eric) taught tennis and strung rackets.

13

FLORIDA KEYS
SHOOTING CLUB
1 GUN CLUB ROAD
KEY LARGO
KEYSSHOOTINGCLUB.COM | (305) 619-3326

THE SCENE
John is doing target practice at this shooting range. He is approached by Eddy, a sheriff and member of the union. John jokingly asks if his union dues don't cover shaving cream. Eddy jokes about John paying his union dues, then stresses the importance of Eric being convicted. They have an awkward encounter where Eddy asks John if he is really okay.

BEHIND THE SCENE
Billed as the Southernmost Shooting Club in the United States, the Florida Keys Shooting Club has a great range tucked away in the outback of Key Largo. The range is open to members and non-members. A shooting schedule can be found on their website.

GETTING THERE
From Overseas Highway, turn onto Central Avenue, Oceanside near Mile Marker 100.7, then turn left on Gun Club Road and follow it until it ends.

FIRST FEATURED
Part 29 | 22:07

FIRE AWAY
Kyle Chandler *(John)* is a volunteer fireman in Dripping Springs, Texas.

14

KEY LARGO FISHERIES
1313 OCEAN BAY DRIVE
KEY LARGO
KEYLARGOFISHERIES.COM | (305) 451-3784

THE SCENE
Eric O'Bannon works here. Detective Marco Diaz confronts Eric at his job as Eric cleans fish guts from dirty buckets. Marco suggests that Eric was at the Red Reef Inn and that he assisted Danny with murder. Eric suggests Marco talks to Danny's family if he wants answers.

BEHIND THE SCENE
In 1972, Jack and Dottie Hill started Jack Hill Bait & Seafood with their two sons and a pick-up truck. By 1976 the business had grown into Key Largo Fisheries. Sitting on five acres of land and water, the fisheries include a marina, retail store, café, and seafood processing facility.

GETTING THERE
Take Ocean Bay Drive off of the Overseas Highway near Mile Marker 100 and continue until you see the marina.

FIRST FEATURED
Part 20| 6:50

TICKET TO RIDE
Jamie McShane *(Eric)* didn't have a car during his stay in the Keys. His transportation was a bicycle with a milk crate on the back of it.

15

PHOTO: RAY GRIMES

MOLASSES REEF
IN THE OCEAN
KEY LARGO
KEYSDIVER.COM | (305) 451-1177

THE SCENE
Season 3, Episode 8 opens with a boat flying its dive flag and rocking gently back and forth over this reef. Later in the episode, John is seen spearfishing and chasing his sister's seahorse necklace. It's a trippy episode that you can interpret yourself, but the boat was at Molasses Reef.

BEHIND THE SCENE
Molasses Reef is a coral reef located within the Florida Keys National Marine Sanctuary. The location is easily identified by the unmanned reef light located nearby. In 1984, a vessel carrying chicken feed ran aground here and settled a claim worth more than $6,000,000 for damage to the reef. Today Molasses Reef remains a popular snorkel and dive spot.

GETTING THERE
Keys Diver offers snorkel trips to Molasses Reef. They are located at 99696 Overseas Highway in Key Largo just off Mile Marker 99.6.

FIRST FEATURED
Part 31 | 1:32

SHOOTING STAR
Kyle Chandler *(John)* had a star near Orion's Belt named for him in 2007.

16

DENNY'S LATIN CAFE
99600 OVERSEAS HIGHWAY
KEY LARGO
(305) 451-3665

THE SCENE

This location was included in the first Bloodline location guide, but is listed again because the significant scene where Ozzy commits suicide was filmed here in season 3. Ozzy is seen here talking to Roy Gilbert on the phone, then sitting in his car with Nolan. The next day he returns to meet Roy, but is greeted by Roy's thugs instead. They lead him to their car and he senses what is going to happen. Ozzy then pulls a gun from his sock and blows his brains out.

BEHIND THE SCENE

Denny's Latin Cafe should not be confused with Denny's just down the road. Denny's Latin Cafe serves up great Latin food with a menu full of favorites. Try the Cuban Coffee and the Cuban Mix Sandwich. Save room for Flan.

GETTING THERE

Watch for the red and yellow awning at Mile Marker 99.6 Bayside. The cafe is open from 6AM to 10PM every day.

FIRST FEATURED

Part 31| 23:20

BLOWN AWAY

John Leguizamo *(Ozzy)* chose to have Ozzy die by committing suicide when show creator Todd Kessler told him the character was coming to an end.

17

PILOT HOUSE
13 SEAGATE BLVD.
KEY LARGO
PILOTHOUSEMARINA.COM | (305) 451-3142

THE SCENE
John drops Nolan off for a job interview. He offers to go in and speak to the owner, but Nolan is offended and says he doesn't need help getting a job as a dishwasher. John looks at Nolan's application and says he is glad he's not the only one Nolan lies to. Nolan gives attitude and heads inside.

BEHIND THE SCENE
The Pilot House is located on Lake Largo and has been a Key Largo landmark since 1950. It is a popular spot with locals, and well known for its glass bottom bar that allows you to see the fish swimming beneath your feet.

GETTING THERE
Located just off Mile Marker 99.5 Oceanside, take Ocean Bay Drive to Seagate Blvd and take a left. The Pilot House will be one of the first places on your right.

FIRST FEATURED
Part 16 | 2:57

BELLE OF THE BALL
Owen Teague *(Nolan)* credits his acting success to Disney's *Beauty and the Beast.* He used to act out the scenes every day when he was four.

18

MRS. MAC'S KITCHEN
99336 OVERSEAS HIGHWAY
KEY LARGO
MRSMACSKITCHEN.COM | (305) 451-3722

THE SCENE
John sits in the corner booth of this restaurant. He and Agent Kimball discuss Kevin being under investigation, and John tries to figure out how he can help Kevin. Agent Kimball asks if Kevin would turn state's witness. John says Kevin would need witness protection.

BEHIND THE SCENE
Mrs. Mac's Kitchen was originally founded by Jeff MacFarland in 1976. He named it in honor of his mother and her recipes. The building was built in 1947 as Grainger's Gulf Side Inn. Today it is a local favorite that regularly wins "best" awards.

GETTING THERE
Mrs. Mac's is located at Mile Marker 99.3 Bayside. The Overseas Highway is split here, so you want to be in the southbound lane to access the restaurant. Watch for the large wooden sign in front of a one-story building with turquoise trim.

FIRST FEATURED
Part 33 | 28:12

OFF LEASH
Kyle Chandler *(John)* met his wife in a dog park.

19

WYLAND'S
WHALING WALL
99216 OVERSEAS HIGHWAY
KEY LARGO

THE SCENE

Kevin is sent to retrieve the dolphin statue he used to kill Marco. He starts to have a nervous breakdown and pulls over in front of this building. After tearing off his shirt, he calls John, who finally picks up. John tells him to stay where he is. Kevin says he is at Mile Marker 80. Lou Reed's Perfect Day plays over the scene with the lyrics, "You're going to reap just what you sow."

BEHIND THE SCENE

Marine life artist Wyland painted 100 "Whaling Wall" murals around the world to promote ocean conservation. The 7500 square-foot mural in Key Largo was his 95th in the series and his last in the United States. The wall was completed in 2007 and includes a stingray as a tribute to Steve Irwin.

GETTING THERE

Look for a colorfully painted building in the median of the Overseas Highway at Mile Marker 92.2.

FIRST FEATURED

Part 25 | 16:20

DOWNSIZING

Bloodline was originally planned to have a five or six season arc.

20

ISLAND GRILL
AT MANDALAY
80 EAST 2ND STREET
KEY LARGO
KEYSISLANDGRILL.COM | (305) 852-0595

THE SCENE
This is the bar where Kevin gets busted. Kevin has fled to Bimini. He is enjoying a beer at the bar when a Bahamian police officer and Nicholas, the DEA agent, show up to arrest him.

BEHIND THE SCENE
The Mandalay has been a Key Largo landmark since 1947 as a shack, a marina, and then a restaurant. It was immortalized by artist Harry Sonntag in the 50s and today hosts an excellent casual dining joint famous for their tuna nachos.

GETTING THERE
Take 2nd Avenue Oceanside near Mile Marker 97.5. It is located next to Shell World and dead ends at Island Grill.

FIRST FEATURED
Part 33 | 103:10

CHOOSE YOUR OWN ADVENTURE
Talking about the series finale, creator Todd Kessler explains, that by that point, the audience should be able to put themselves in the shoes of the characters and decide what happens.

21

DAIRY QUEEN
92661 OVERSEAS HIGHWAY
TAVERNIER
(305) 852-2219

THE SCENE
After being beaten, a bloodied Ozzy walks into this "Creamy King" and asks if the Polar Freeze is the one that makes your tongue turn blue. The young man behind the counter is freaked out by the blood on Ozzy's face. Ozzy orders a large.

BEHIND THE SCENE
This Dairy Queen serves food and ice cream. In August of 2017, two people scarier than Ozzy came in and robbed the place at gunpoint.

GETTING THERE
Located at Mile Marker 92.6 in the median. Watch for the red oval sign.

FIRST FEATURED
Part 25 | 30:16

TALK THE TALK
John Leguizamo (Ozzy) was voted "Most Talkative" by his classmates at Murry Bergtraum High School.

22

HARRY HARRIS PARK
50 BEACH ROAD
TAVERNIER
(305) 852-7161

THE SCENE
John sits in his truck at this park with Sheriff Aguirre. He says he doesn't need to be read his rights and that he is here to confess. He then says that he is responsible for his brother's death and for framing Eric. Aguirre refuses his confession and reveals he is going to work with Mike Gallagher. He also tells John that Belle forgot to turn off the GPS on her phone and that Kevin is being brought in.

BEHIND THE SCENE
Harry Harris Park is an oceanfront park with pavilions, barbecues, picnic tables, basketball, baseball, and playgrounds. It is named after a former county commissioner.

GETTING THERE
From Mile Marker 92.6 take Burton Drive to East Beach Road. $5 per person admission for non-residents on holidays and weekends.

FIRST FEATURED
Part 33 | 59:10

ANIMAL FARM
Kyle Chandler *(John)* has four dogs and five miniature donkeys.

23

MILE MARKER 88
TO
MILE MARKER 91.6

KEVIN'S
GUNPOINT DRIVE
OVERSEAS HIGHWAY
TAVERNIER

THE SCENE

Kevin gets in his truck. A Cuban hiding in the backseat pulls a gun on him, and demands to know what he told Nicholas. Kevin is freaking out. The Cuban reveals that Nicholas is a Fed, then demands a boat and threatens to kill Kevin's son.

BEHIND THE SCENE

This tense drive took place through Tavernier heading north from just before Mile Marker 88 to Mile Marker 91.6. Kevin lets the Cuban out of the car in front of the Florida Keys Electric Cooperative. The name Tavernier may have evolved in part from the Spanish "Tabona," meaning "horsefly."

GETTING THERE

Stay on the Overseas Highway and drive from Mile Marker 88 to Mile Marker 91.6. Keep a close watch on the backseat of your car.

FIRST FEATURED

Part 33 | 6:27

MORE, MORE, MORE!

Fans of Bloodline started an online petition demanding a 4th season of the show. The petition has nearly 2000 signatures.

24

PHOTO: JANIE HOWARD GOLDEN

TOILET SEAT CUT
OFFSHORE
TAVERNIER

THE SCENE

No scene was filmed here, but it is quirky location with a cool piece of Bloodline history attached to it. Toilet Seat Cut is named for the dozens of toilet seats mounted to channel markers that people have decorated to commemorate weddings, birthdays, and other special events. After filming wrapped for season 3, the Bloodline crew decorated their own seat and added it to Toilet Seat Cut.

BEHIND THE SCENE

The tradition of hanging toilet seats on the channel markers started after one toilet seat ended up here accidentally during Hurricane Donna in 1960.

GETTING THERE

Kayaks can be rented nearby from Paddle! The Florida Keys *(paddlethefloridakeys.com).* 90773 Old Highway, (305) 434-5930

FIRST FEATURED

Not featured, but cool.

FRAMED

The art of Florida Keys artist, Dan Lawler, is featured in many Bloodline scenes. Dan has been a Keys resident for more than 50 years.

25

OLD TAVERNIER
90311 OLD HIGHWAY
TAVERNIER
(305) 852-6012

THE SCENE
Eve meets Ozzy here and he gives her a stack of cash. Ozzy wants her to come with him, but Eve reveals that she and Nolan are staying at the Rayburn Inn. Ozzy is angry and accuses her of working the situation. Meg drives by and sees them together. Eve breaks up with Ozzy.

BEHIND THE SCENE
Established in 1988, The Old Tavernier restaurant is popular with locals and tourists for both Greek and Italian food. People rave about the pizza, but it is only served in the bar. Take your date here if you want to break up with them like Eve did.

GETTING THERE
Look for the green awning that says "Restaurant" on a building set back over a red-bricked parking lot with flags flying by the road near Mile Marker 90.3.

FIRST FEATURED
Part 22 | 45:40

PUNCH BOWL
John Leguizamo *(Ozzy)* grew up in a neighborhood with a lot of fights. He says it inspired him to be funny so he didn't get hit.

26

CORAL SHORES
HIGH SCHOOL
89901 OLD HIGHWAY
TAVERNIER

THE SCENE
Eve surprises John's daughter Jane by appearing outside of her high school. Jane says she has a lot of homework. Eve says she has a lot of questions.

BEHIND THE SCENE
In 1951 the school Superintendent asked citizens of the Upper Keys to submit names for a new school. Sally Jinette of Greyhound Key submitted the name "Coral Shores" which was chosen as the winner. The school opened with six teachers and six classrooms for grades one through eleven.

GETTING THERE
Coral Shores is located at Mile Marker 89.9 Oceanside. Watch for the concrete building with the light green accents.

FIRST FEATURED
Part 19 | 19:02

DOG DAYS
Taylor Rouviere *(Jane)* participates actively in dog rescue. She has seven dogs of her own and rescued several abandoned dogs in Homestead, Florida, during the filming of Bloodline.

27

SAN PEDRO CHURCH
89500 OVERSEAS HIGHWAY
TAVERNIER
SANPEDROPARISH.ORG | (305) 852-5372

THE SCENE

Kevin and Belle host the christening of their baby, Rocky, at this church. In the scene, John has not arrived to fulfill his duties as godfather. Kevin asks longtime family friend Roy Gilbert to step in. Scenes were also filmed in the garden here with Sally taking to the priest and wanting to confess.

BEHIND THE SCENE

Fittingly named for Saint Peter, a fisherman, the San Pedro Roman Catholic Church was dedicated in 1955. The bins at the entrance are built from ballast stone from the wreck of the San Pedro, part of the 1733 Treasure Fleet. The communion bell was once used in a small Mexican Chapel, and the tower bell was cast in 1917. Many lighting fixture are copies of the Majano lanterns of Rome.

GETTING THERE

The church is set back from the highway at Mile Marker 89.5, Bayside. Look for the church sign closer to the highway, and a statue of San Pedro midway to the church.

FIRST FEATURED

Part 27 | 47:00

THE NAME GAME

Lloyd Vernet Bridges III *(Roy)* was nicknamed Beau by his parents after Ashley Wilkes' son in *Gone With The Wind*.

28

BALI HAI
89301 OLD HIGHWAY
TAVERNIER
PRIVATE RESIDENCE

THE SCENE
This is Roy Gilbert's House. We first see it when John is running for sheriff, and John and Meg come here to win Gilbert's favor. They pitch their campaign strategy, then have an awkward moment talking about John and Meg's father.

BEHIND THE SCENE
Bali Hai is the home of Jon and Julie Landau. Jon Landau is the Academy Award winning producer behind *Avatar* and *Titanic*. The property covers four acres, including 200 feet of oceanfront. It has 7 bedrooms and 5.5 bathrooms.

GETTING THERE
The best way to see this property is from the water or with an invitation from the Landaus. It is located at Mile Marker 89.3 Oceanside. The area is known as Millionaire's Row.

FIRST FEATURED
Part 18 | 24:32

GRAB BAG
"I wanted to finally get all of their property, and maybe even get their mother to come over to me. Something that I've wanted all of my life."
– *Beau Bridges speaking on Roy Gilbert's motives.*

29

MONROE COUNTY DETENTION CENTER
53 HIGH POINT RD
TAVERNIER
KEYSSO.NET | (305) 853-3266

THE SCENE
This is the detention center where Eric is being held. John pulls into the parking lot and a deputy comes to his truck. John hands him an envelope and says, "Thanks for that." He is referring to making Eric miss his mother's funeral. The deputy replies, "Whatever you need, Detective." John pulls away.

BEHIND THE SCENE
Monroe County has had 36 sheriffs since it was incorporated in 1823. Today, the office operates three correctional facilities in the Florida Keys. The Plantation Key Detention Center can hold 47 prisoners. This is a location that is better to see from the outside than the inside.

GETTING THERE
The Plantation Key Detention Center is located just off Mile Marker 88.8 Bayside. Turn onto High Point Road next to Jersey Boardwalk Pizza. The detention center will be on your left.

FIRST FEATURED
Part 27 | 52:25

PUCK OFF
Jaime McShane *(Eric)* had a dream of playing hockey in the Olympics. His dream was cut short by a head injury.

30

MONROE COUNTY
PLANTATION KE
GOVERNMENT CENTER
CLERKS OFFICE
COURT ROOMS
JUDGES CHAMBERS
STATE ATTORNEY OFFICE
CATHERINE VOGEL

PLANTATION KEY COURTHOUSE

88820 OVERSEAS HIGHWAY

TAVERNIER

THE SCENE
Eric O'Bannon's murder trial takes place here. There are several scenes with the prosecution making him look guilty, and Eric looking defenseless.

BEHIND THE SCENE
The exterior shot opening this scene shows the Florida City Hall dressed up as the Plantation Key Courthouse. The interior scenes were filmed in Tavernier and featured many locals as members of the audience or jury.

GETTING THERE
The Courthouse is located just off Mile Marker 88.8 Bayside. This is a functioning courthouse. You might be better off staying outside and just knowing where it is.

FIRST FEATURED
Part 29 | 14:30

PACK RAT
After college, Jamie *(Eric)* worked three jobs until he saved enough money to backpack around the world.

31

FOUNDER'S PARK
AMPHITHEATER
87000 OVERSEAS HIGHWAY
ISLAMORADA
(305) 664-6400

THE SCENE
Marco's funeral takes place here. The scene starts with Sally calling Meg. A priest and several members of law enforcement gather. The mood is somber. The Rayburns give hugs to the Diaz family. Marco's casket is brought in. John delivers a eulogy.

BEHIND THE SCENE
Founders Park is the location for several Bloodline scenes. The amphitheater hosts regular concerts and community events. Even the Norbert Leo Butz Band played there. Casting calls for this scene requested as many real law enforcement officers as possible. Many answered the call.

GETTING THERE
Founders Park is located at Mile Marker 87 Bayside. The amphitheater is located at the back of the park just past the swimming pool.

FIRST FEATURED
Part 27 | 3:40

LAND OF PLENTY
"There's always more bodies."
– Show creator, Todd Kessler

32

FOUNDER'S PARK
87000 OVERSEAS HIGHWAY
ISLAMORADA
(305) 664-6400

THE SCENE
Diana Rayburn is jogging in the park by the beach. She returns to her car to find a flat tire. Ozzy appears and asks if she needs help. He offers her a beer, spots a "Rayburn For Sheriff" bumper sticker on her car, and asks Diana if she is voting for John Rayburn. Diana says she is his wife. Ozzy then teases that information he knows could derail John's campaign.

BEHIND THE SCENE
Founders Park was used in multiple Bloodline scenes including baseball games and funerals. This part of the park is actually popular for jogging, though not a lot of flat tires happen here.

GETTING THERE
Founders Park is located at Mile Marker 87 Bayside. Stay to your left as you enter the park and you will get to the beach, playground, and picnic parking area. This is the parking lot where the scene was filmed.

FIRST FEATURED
Part 19 | 19:45

HOT TO TROT
Jacinda Barrett *(Diana)* was chosen by People Magazine as one of the 50 Most Beautiful People In the World.

33

MARCO'S HOUSE
115 TONER LANE
ISLAMORADA
PRIVATE RESIDENCE

THE SCENE
Marco's house appears in many episodes. We first see it when Meg visits him and confesses that her family is a mess. The most memorable scene filmed here involved Kevin beating Marco to death with a dolphin statue.

BEHIND THE SCENE
The house contains 1200 square feet and was built in 1958. It contains two bedrooms and two bathrooms. It last sold in 2009 for $330,000. Today it is worth just over half a million dollars.

GETTING THERE
Take East Ridge Road off the Old Highway near Mile Marker 87 Oceanside. East Ridge Road leads to Toner Lane. The house is at the end of the road. This is a private residence. Please do not disturb occupants.

FIRST FEATURED
Part 20 | 42:21

NEED FOR SPEED
Enrique Murciano *(Marco)* made his feature film debut in the 1997 action film Speed 2: Cruise Control.

34

HARBOR LIGHTS MOTEL
84951 OVERSEAS HIGHWAY
ISLAMORADA
HARBORLIGHTSFLORIDA.COM | (305) 664-3611

THE SCENE

This is the motel where John has been staying since separating from his wife after she learned that he killed his brother. Several scenes take place here. In the first, John is taking a shower. In another scene, his wife shows up drunk and, like a good husband, he tucks her into bed and sleeps on the couch. In another scene, he sleeps with his new partner here. A former colleague and friend also finds him here and questions his lifestyle.

BEHIND THE SCENE

Harbor Lights is a 30-room motel located on Windley Key in Islamorada. It used to be a part of Holiday Isle. Just as Bloodline was finishing up filming, the property sold for a reported $7,000,000. The place is undergoing a complete renovation that is scheduled to be finished in early 2018 when the resort will open as The Fisher Inn. John Rayburn stayed in room 20.

GETTING THERE

Harbor Lights is located at Mile Marker 84.9 Oceanside in Islamorada.

FIRST FEATURED

Part 27 | 27:11

CH-CH-CH-CH CHANGES

In 1994, The New York Times said of Chandler (John), "His boyish demeanor and unimposing physique make it impossible to think of him as a hunk,"

35

POSTCARD INN MARINA
84001 OVERSEAS HIGHWAY
ISLAMORADA
HOLIDAYISLE.COM | (305) 664-2321

THE SCENE
A large molded shark dominates the screen as Nolan walks across the marina parking lot to meet his mother, Evangeline. He gets in her car and she asks him if the Rayburns are treating him all right. He says they are. She gives him a kiss on the cheek.

BEHIND THE SCENE
Islamorada is known as the Sport Fishing Capital of the World. The Postcard Inn Marina hosts the famous fishing fleet of Holiday Isle. They even have a chalkboard in the main lobby where you can boast about the size of your catch. The Rum Runner was invented on this property too.

GETTING THERE
The marina is located at Mile Marker 84 on the south side of the Postcard Inn property. Watch for the area with a lot of boats.

FIRST FEATURED
Part 16 | 45:49

THE YOUNG & THE RESTLESS
Owen Teague *(Nolan)* played a young Danny in flashback scenes during season one of Bloodline.

36

WHALE HARBOR
CHAIN GANG
84001 OVERSEAS HIGHWAY
ISLAMORADA

THE SCENE

Eric is working with a prison road crew. John approaches him and says he is there to confess. Eric tells him to go fuck himself in hell. As the conversation continues, Eric asks John to keep Nolan out of it, saying that Nolan doesn't need to know that John killed his father. A prison guard interrupts and tells Eric to get back to work.

BEHIND THE SCENE

There is not much exciting about a side stretch of highway normally, but back when Henry Flagler's railroad was running, the strip of land where Eric is working was the original Overseas Highway. Whale Harbor is where Meg says Sarah drowned.

GETTING THERE

This scene was filmed just north of the Whale Harbor Bridge Oceanside near Mile Marker 84. The strip of land is between the Postcard Inn and Whale Harbor Bridge.

FIRST FEATURED

Part 33 | 3:59

CANDY LAND

Jamie McShane's *(Eric)* favorite candy is chocolate covered caramels from Trader Joe's.

37

ACE HARDWARE
82905 OVERSEAS HIGHWAY
ISLAMORADA
(305) 664-8823

THE SCENE
Kevin goes into "Reef Hardware" looking for paint for the baby's room. A store employee asks him if it should be pink or blue paint, then suggests pale green. The employee reveals that he recognizes Kevin from their AA meetings. He writes down his number on a card, offering to help if Kevin ever needs anything. Kevin is resistant.

BEHIND THE SCENE
There is no Home Depot in Islamorada, so we are still blessed with the benefits of a true local hardware store. This scene was filmed in the center aisle, but if you go in today, that is not where you will find the paint. The store was rearranged to accommodate filming.

GETTING THERE
Ace is located at Mile Marker 82.9 Oceanside. Look for the Ace sign and the tropical mural painted across the building.

FIRST FEATURED
Part 19 | 13:50

RISE & SHINE
Norbert Leo Butz *(Kevin)* says he literally didn't sleep for three days after reading the season two finale script.

38

THE PRODUCTION LOT
82779 OLD HIGHWAY
ISLAMORADA

THE SCENE
No scenes were filmed here, but this lot was the heart of operations during the filming of Bloodline. The stars had their trailers here. All of the cast and crew were fed here. Extras reported here to get wardrobe for their scenes.

BEHIND THE SCENE
This is one of the few undeveloped lots in Islamorada that could handle the production demands of Bloodline.

GETTING THERE
The lot is located at the end of DeLeon Avenue, just behind the post office off Mile Marker 82.7 Oceanside. This is private property. Not much to see, but a cool location for fans who want to see where the backbone of the show was located.

FIRST FEATURED
Cast & crew location only.

ANOTHER ONE RIDES THE BUS
Cast and crew were transported to film locations by shuttle buses that picked them up in the lot behind the post office.

39

CORAL BAY MARINA
601 MASTIC STREET
ISLAMORADA
CORAL-BAY-MARINA.COM | (305) 664-3111

THE SCENE
Called Indian Key Channel Marina in the series, locals know it as Coral Bay Marina. Fans of the show know it as Kevin Rayburn's marina and office where he can be seen snorting lots of cocaine and generally melting down. This is also the site where Kevin and Danny work to restore their father's old Chevy truck in Season 1.

BEHIND THE SCENE
Coral Bay is a full-service working marina established in 1983. They have 30+ wet slips for transient and live-aboard customers and onsite mechanics for all types of boat services.

GETTING THERE
The marina is open Monday – Friday from 8AM – 4:30PM, and in the summer, 7AM – 3:30PM. This is a working marina. Consider parking in the parking lot of the family owned Trading Post, open 24 hours, at Mile Marker 82, Bayside. Belle's Boutique is located here, as is a restaurant frequented by cast and crew, Bad Boy Burrito.

FIRST FEATURED
Featured often.

KEYS PLEASE
"I'm unabashed in my love and loyalty for the Florida Keys. I will be returning there long after Bloodline."
– *Norbert Leo Butz (Kevin)*

40

WOODY'S
81908 OVERSEAS HIGHWAY
ISLAMORADA
(305) 664-4335

THE SCENE

Kevin gets suckered into taking the Cuban smugglers out a second time and they go to this strip club. The Cubans cut lines of cocaine on the table. Kevin goes to the bathroom and looks at a photo of his son to help keep his senses. A fight breaks out in the bar with a dancer and the cops are called. A waitress tells John that his brother was involved.

BEHIND THE SCENE

Woody's is an actual strip club. It is the only strip club in the Keys outside of Key West. They feature a full liquor bar and full nudity. The facade on the building would lead you to believe that the name is derived from the vintage "Woody" wagon.

GETTING THERE

Woody's is located at Mile Marker 81.9 Bayside in a single-story structure with a Woody on the side.

FIRST FEATURED

Part 28 | 38:12

YIN & YANG

Norbert Leo Butz *(Kevin)* once called himself "the most successful unsuccessful actor in New York."

41

OCEAN SOTHEBY'S
INTERNATIONAL REALTY
81888 OVERSEAS HIGHWAY
ISLAMORADA

THE SCENE
This is Sheriff Aguirre's campaign headquarters. Meg meets Aguirre's campaign manager here to discuss terms of the debate. As she is leaving, Meg encounters Ozzy. He threatens to tell the sheriff everything he knows and laughs that she thinks she is the victim. Ozzy tells her that one way or another, their conversation ends in 24 hours.

BEHIND THE SCENE
The strip plaza where this scene was filmed includes Ocean Sotheby's, Islamorada Investment Management. and Roberto Russell Galleries. It is located close to the marina depicted as Kevin's.

GETTING THERE
Watch for the yellow building set back from the road at Mile Marker 81.8 on Blackwood Drive.

FIRST FEATURED
Part 21 | 26:20

COP OUT
David Zayas *(Sheriff Aguirre)* was a NYPD beat cop in Time Square. He is the only cast member of *Dexter* who was an actual police officer.

42

PIONEER CEMETERY
AT CHEECA LODGE
81801 OVERSEAS HIGHWAY
ISLAMORADA
CHEECA.COM | (305) 712-7166

THE SCENE

This is the cemetery where Danny is buried. Eric O'Bannon drinks a beer here and smokes a joint. He flashes back to memories of being shot at in the Red Reef Inn then finding Danny with a bloody conch shell in hand.

BEHIND THE SCENE

Though the beach with the cemetery now belongs to Cheeca Lodge, it was once part of the community of Matecumbe. In the early 1900s, this was where the Matecumbe Methodist Church and the Matecumbe School were located. Both were destroyed by the 1935 Labor Day Hurricane. The cemetery survived, with the exception of an angel who lost one of her wings in the storm.

GETTING THERE

Cheeca Lodge is located Oceanside at Mile Marker 81.8, directly across the street from The Trading Post. Let the guard gate know you are visiting the cemetery or coming for lunch. Head toward the ocean and stick to your right to find the cemetery.

FIRST FEATURED

Part 14 | 16:51

BREAKFAST IS SERVED

"Ben approaches every scene with the simple motto of 'making the first pancake.'" He says, "We all have to flip the first one before the others can be made."
– *Todd Kessler*

43

PHOTO: ANCHORED MEDIA

MOORINGS VILLIAGE
123 BEACH ROAD
ISLAMORADA
THEMOORINGSVILLAGE.COM | (305) 664-4708

THE SCENE
The waterfront hotel owned by Robert and Sally Rayburn is featured regularly, hosting everything from a funeral to a family reunion.

BEHIND THE SCENE
The property was originally home to the Matecumbe Club, constructed in 1919 for the exclusive use of 11 members of the New York Cotton Exchange. Destroyed in the 1935 Labor Day Hurricane, reconstruction began in 1936 with the building of a private residence and several outlying buildings. The area was devastated again by Hurricane Donna in 1960. Ralph Edsell, Sr., rebuilt, constructing a small beachside resort. Long time locals still refer to the beach here as Scudders Beach. The property was upgraded in the late 1980s with the addition of 14 cottages.

GETTING THERE
The property is only accessible to guests of the resort. If you are not a guest, save yourself the trouble of being turned away without seeing anything. Instead, rent a paddleboard or kayak from Cheeca Lodge, paddle by, and check out the great view of the property from the water.

FIRST FEATURED
Multiple episodes. Primary set.

SLEEP LIKE THE RAYBURNS
The Blue Charlotte House, home to the Rayburn clan, is a three-bedroom, 6500 square foot home at Moorings Village available for about $2500 per night.

44

PHOTO: FISHBONE

FISHBONE
FISHING CHARTERS
81576 OVERSEAS HIGHWAY
ISLAMORADA
FISHBONEFISHING.COM | (305) 394-5305

THE SCENE

As a favor to Roy, Kevin takes three Cuban drug smugglers fishing in this boat. Kevin tells them how his father taught him about the importance of a fair fight with the fish. The Cubans hook a blue marlin and ask Kevin to use the engines. He says no. A moment later one of the Cubans pulls out a gun and shoots the fish.

BEHIND THE SCENE

Fishbone is a 2004 65-foot Custom Island Boat Works powered by two Caterpillar C30 engines. It has four twin beds and one master bedroom, two full baths and one half-bath, plus a roomy salon, satellite TV, and a fighting chair.

GETTING THERE

Fishbone Fishing Charters is located behind World Wide Sportsman in Islamorada at Mile Marker 81.5 Bayside. Watch for the large brick structure and the packed parking lot.

FIRST FEATURED

Part 28 | 18:19

LOCAL COLOR

Many Florida Keys residents were cast as extras in Bloodline. Standard pay was $112.70 for up to 12 hours.

45

BANYAN TREE
81197 OVERSEAS HIGHWAY
ISLAMORADA
BANYANTREEBOUTIQUE.COM | (305) 664-3433

THE SCENE
Jane Rayburn tries on a blouse in this boutique. Eve asks her if she has ever modeled, then reveals she is a singer. Jane says she can't afford the blouse and that her parents would kill her. Eve offers to put it back for her, but we later find out that she shoplifts it.

BEHIND THE SCENE
Banyan Tree is a local favorite, owned and operated by mother and daughter, Robin and Pauline. The boutique has unique gifts, amazing jewelry, and a collection of nature-inspired women's clothing and accessories. The grounds for the garden and boutique include a large banyan tree, and the garden overflows with orchids and other plants, all of which are for sale.

GETTING THERE
The Banyan Tree is located at Mile Marker 81.1 Oceanside just across the street from the Kon Tiki Resort. Watch for the white picket fence, pink sign, and banyan tree.

FIRST FEATURED
Part 19 | 20:29

RETURN TO SENDER
9000 Bloodline items including props, furniture, clothing, and accessories were auctioned after the series ended. The Banyan Tree scored the blouse that was "stolen" from their store. It is now on display.

46

PALMS OF
ISLAMORADA
79901 OVERSEAS HIGHWAY
ISLAMORADA

THE SCENE
These are the condominiums where it is revealed that Kevin has been set up by the DEA while overseeing a major drug deal with the Cubans as a favor to Roy. One of the Cubans, Nicholas, is actually DEA.

BEHIND THE SCENE
Palms of Islamorada is a gated condominium complex located directly on the Atlantic Ocean. Many of the units are rented on a monthly basis for $2200 - $3900.

GETTING THERE
The complex is gated, so this is more of a drive-by location. Who wants to go to a place with a bunch of DEA agents, anyway? Watch for the beige three-story building at Mile Marker 79.9 Oceanside.

FIRST FEATURED
Part 31 | 46:51

ROLE CALL
Josue Gutierrez *(Nicholas)* has also appeared in Homeland, Drop Dead Diva, Under The Dome, and Twilight.

47

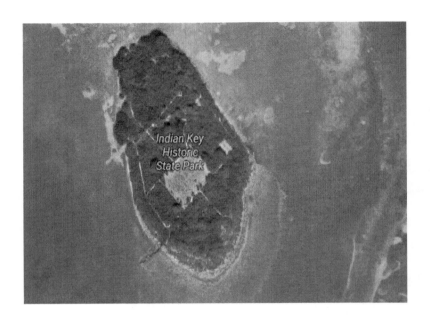

Indian Key Historic State Park

INDIAN KEY
77522 OVERSEAS HIGHWAY
ISLAMORADA

THE SCENE

Eric stashes gas cans here for the human smugglers. The island is also used as a base of operations for the special effects crew when they blow up the smuggler's boat. The waters off island are where they filmed Sarah Rayburn losing her seahorse necklace, getting her hand stuck in the coral, and drowning.

BEHIND THE SCENE

The 11-acre island was home to a thriving wrecking village in the 1830s where residents made their wealth salvaging ships that wrecked on the nearby reef. In 1840 the island was attacked by a large party of Native Americans in what has become known as "The Indian Key Massacre." Today the island is a state park and the only ghost town in the Florida Keys.

GETTING THERE

Accessible only by boat or kayak, Indian Key is a one-mile paddle from Robbie's Marina. Entry is just $2.50. Kayaks can be rented from Florida Keys Kayak at Robbie's Marina.

FIRST FEATURED

Part 1 | 57.58

MODEL CITIZEN

Angela Winiewicz *(Sarah)* began her modeling career when she was four months old and started acting when she was two. She likes swimming and climbing trees.

48

PHOTO: STEVE CARR

ERIC'S HIDEOUT
77522 OVERSEAS HIGHWAY
ISLAMORADA
ROBBIES.COM | (877) 664-8498

THE SCENE
Eric hides in this shack after being framed for Marco's murder. John Rayburn finds him here, and a frightened Eric claims his innocence. John gives Marco's gun to Eric. Eric tries to shoot John but there are no bullets. John tosses Eric a bag with money and clothes. He said he's only been here once. They both credit Danny with showing them the location. John throws a pocketful of bullets in Eric's direction and wishes him luck.

BEHIND THE SCENE
Eric's Hideout is actually a residence for employees of Robbie's. It is in an off-limits area, but can be seen from the water by kayak.

GETTING THERE
Rent a kayak from the Kayak Shack at Robbie's Marina and head to your left. Stick to the shoreline around the mainland and you will see the houses, shacks, and boats.

FIRST FEATURED
Part 26 | 39:08

PUT ME IN COACH
Kyle Chandler *(John)* voiced the role of a coach in *Family Guy, American Dad, and Monstrous Holiday*. He also played Coach Taylor in *Friday Night Lights*.

49

CALOOSA COVE TIKI
73801 OVERSEAS HIGHWAY
ISLAMORADA
CALOOSACOVE.COM | (305) 664-8811

THE SCENE
Marco meets Meg at this Tiki. He brings up his family birthday party, and tells how disappointed he was—not with Meg, but with himself. He says he has been an idiot and then proposes by saying, "Let's get fucking married, okay?" He then leans in to kiss her. She kisses him back.

BEHIND THE SCENE
Caloosa Cove Resort and Marina is located on 15 tropical acres in Islamorada. The resort included 30 oceanfront suites, a full-service marina, fishing charters, island store, restaurants, and a bar. The name "Caloosa" comes from the Caloosa Indians who once roamed the Keys.

GETTING THERE
Watch for the Safari Lounge sign with the big rhino at Mile Marker 73.8 Oceanside. Follow the road back past the bar and you will see the Tiki where Marco proposed directly in front of you.

FIRST FEATURED
Part 8 | 26:33

HOT TO TROT
"The sweat on us all is real."
— *Linda Cardellini*

50

LONG KEY
TRANSFER STATION
68521 OVERSEAS HIGHWAY
LAYTON

THE SCENE
The Rayburn siblings, John, Meg, and Kevin meet on this dirt road to discuss what has happened. John tells them that Marco has been cleared by the Sheriff's office. Kevin points out that he and Meg had nothing to do with Danny's death. John gets angry and points out that they moved the body. They all argue.

BEHIND THE SCENE
This scene was filmed at the Long Key Transfer Station, a place that deals with garbage, operated by Waste Management. The location is not accessible to the general public, but we have included it because so many people asked where it was.

GETTING THERE
The Long Key Transfer Station is located at Mile Marker 68.5 Bayside, but you can only drive in so far before you are stopped. The best way to see this location is Google Earth.

FIRST FEATURED
Part 23 | 33:00

DEATH & TAXES
Bloodline was cancelled after Florida eliminated their tax credits. Bloodline was the last show to receive the credits.

EAT

DRINK

SLEEP

REFUEL

SHOP

RELAX

BLOODLINE

Neighborhood Notification

The Netflix Original Series *BLOODLINE* will be filming in your neighborhood on **Monday, February 6th, 2017.**

BLOODLINE is a psychological thriller drama set in the Florida Keys. The stellar cast includes Sissy Spacek (an Academy Award Winner & three time Golden Globe Award Winner for Best Actress), Kyle Chandler, (2015 and 2016 Emmy Award Nominee for "Bloodline") Ben Mendelsohn, (2015 Emmy Award Nominee and 2016 Emmy Award Winner for "Bloodline") Norbert Leo Butz, (Two time Tony Award Winner for best actor in a musical), and John Leguizamo. *BLOODLINE* is produced by Sony Pictures and airs on Netflix.

The Filming Information is as follows:
Location:
Harbor Lights, 84951 Overseas Highway, Islamorada, FL 33036, MM 84 Oceanside

Filming Dates & Times: (Times may change)

- Prep: Friday, February 3rd, 2017 – Times: 9AM-6PM
- Shoot: Monday, February 6th, 2017 Times: 6AM-10PM
- Wrap: Tuesday, February 7th, 2017 Times: 9AM-6PM

Additional Information:

- We will drop a lane of traffic on old highway (300 feet) directly outside the aforementioned property, on the northbound lane to park our production vehicles. We will have a police officer on site to assist with local traffic and our production vehicles.
- We will have Monroe County Sheriff's Dept. Deputies on site at all times to assist with local traffic. We will not block any access to homes at any time.

We believe it is a privilege to film in your neighborhood and we shall do all possible to minimize any inconvenience and respect your privacy. For any questions or concerns please contact Jamil Gonzalez, Assistant Location Manager at 6▮▮▮▮▮▮▮ r Location Office a▮▮▮▮▮▮▮▮3

BLOODLINE Season 3 is working closely with the Village of Islamorada regarding our filming activities and logistics. To verify our project, please contact Village of Islamorada at 305-853-1685.

MAY WE TOGETHER HAVE A SUCCESSFUL FILMING EXPERIENCE IN YOUR COMMUNITY

HOT SPOTS TOUR

A LOCAL'S GUIDE TO

BLOODLINE

50 FAMOUS FILM LOCATIONS IN THE FLORIDA KEYS

TOUR BOOK AND LOCATION GUIDE

**CHECK OUT 50 MORE FAMOUS BLOODLINE
LOCATIONS IN THE SEASON 1 & 2 BOOK.
AVAILABLE LOCALLY AND ON AMAZON AND KINDLE**

BRAD BERTELLI

Brad Bertelli is an author, historian and tour guide. He has published six books on Florida and Florida Keys history, curates the Islamorada museum, Keys History & Discovery Center, and operates Historic Upper Keys Walking Tours. His bi-weekly column, Notes on Keys History, appears in The Reporter.

Contact: brad@bradbertelli.com

DAVID SLOAN

David Sloan moved to the Florida Keys in 1996. He is the author of 18 books including Quit Your Job and Move to Key West and The Key West Bucket List. Sloan also runs the popular ghost tour and ghost hunt company, Haunted Key West, and co-produces the Key Lime Festival and the Zero K Cow Key Channel Bridge Run.

Contact david@phantompress.com

ALSO BY DAVID L. SLOAN

ALSO BY BRAD BERTELLI

A LOCAL'S GUIDE TO BLOODLINE

SNORKELING THE FLORIDA KEYS

SNORKELING FLORIDA

ISLAMORADA

KEY LARGO

INDIAN KEY

WHAT THE HALIBUT?

Sally Rayburn is making ceviche for Marco's wake and asks if Cubans make their ceviche with halibut. Halibut is a cold-water fish more likely to be found in Alaska. A true Conch knows ceviche would be made with a local fish such as grouper or snapper.

77931085R00066

Made in the USA
Columbia, SC
07 October 2017